By Chas Addams

FAVORITE HAUNTS

Simon and Schuster   New York

Library of Congress Cataloging in Publication Data

Addams, Charles, date.
  Chas. Addams favorite haunts.

  *Consists of drawings which appeared chiefly in the
New Yorker, 1946-1976.*
    1. American wit and humor, Pictorial. I. Title.
NC1429.A25A418   741.5'973   76-41359

ISBN 0-671-22429-8

"Goodness, no! Our names are Frank and Bob Finley."

"*Looks like the small investor is finally getting back into the market.*"

"*I thought it was me, but maybe the school's no damn good.*"

"Damn you and your cheap Japanese lighters!"

YOU ARE
HERE

"They don't exorcise ghosts the way they used to."

"Is there someone else, Narcissus?"

"But how can I be sure *it's not just for my money?"*

"*Albert! You've gone and blown another fuse!*"

"*When I said you were allowed one phone call, I did not mean*
another *obscene one.*"

"I don't see that our situation is especially improved."

"*Charm bracelets.*"

"It's going to be tough to top that."

"*Sometimes I wish this family had never heard of the*
'Guinness Book of World Records.' "

"Check this one in the rulebook, Rutherford."

"Hold it! For all we know, he may be making a
citizen's arrest."

"Stop me, sire, if you've heard this one."

*"I danced the best I could, but what the guy really has is an
iron deficiency."*

"*Looks like R. & D. is into something big.*"

"There are no great men, my boy—only great committees."

"We'll take it."

"Western Union. Candygram."

"Is John Philip Sousa O.K.?"

"Why can't you be more like Oedipus?"

"Occasionally."

"... as we approach the termination of this semester, we
think you will be gratified to know that your son is
emerging as a real human being."

"It's a boy!"

"Put them in a bag, please. We're taking them home
to the bird."

"*You're a disgrace to all lemmings!*"

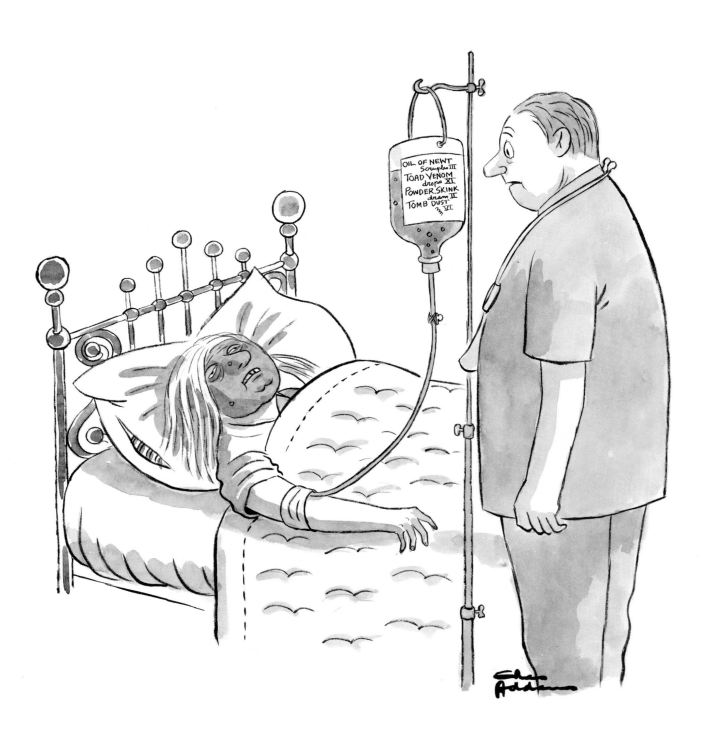

"We're still waiting for Stanley to jell."